POSTCARD HISTORY SERIES

Mount Rainier National Park

FRONT COVER: The description on the card reads as follows: "Henry M. Jackson Memorial Visitor Center, Mt. Rainier, Washington. Located in the Paradise area of Mount Rainier, this visitor center's architecture relates closely to the environment as evidenced in the conical mountain shape of the building, the branching 'tree' columns, 'switch-back trail' ramps, swooping bough-like shaped beams, and the sloped 'cliffs' of the stone base. It is constructed of wood, natural rock and concrete." (Photograph by Richard Johnson.)

BACK COVER: This c. 1908 view of the Longmire Springs Hotel and Spa shows Rampart Ridge to the left, and the Nisqually Road to Parais would be to the right, as would be the National Park Inn. The Longmire Springs Hotel burned down in 1910, and the family operated the spa until 1916. (Courtesy of Linda Lewis.)

POSTCARD HISTORY SERIES

Mount Rainier National Park

Donald M. Johnstone

ARCADIA
PUBLISHING

Published by Arcadia Publishing
Charleston, South Carolina

Printed in the United States of America

Library of Congress Control Number: 2012945567

For all general information contact Arcadia Publishing at:
Telephone 843-853-2070
Fax 843-853-0044
E-mail sales@arcadiapublishing.com
For customer service and orders:
Toll-Free 1-888-313-2665

Visit us on the Internet at www.arcadiapublishing.com

This book is dedicated to the women and men who have devoted their time, love, attention, careers, and sometimes lives to the preservation of America's natural places.

CONTENTS

ACKNOWLEDGMENTS

A work such as this owes much to many contributors. I have attempted to acknowledge the provider of each image at the caption. Extraordinary thanks go to Rick Johnson and Jana Gardiner of Ashford Creek Pottery and Gallery in Ashford, Washington. In the shop, Rick displays his collection of nearly 1,000 postcards of Mount Rainier–related scenes. Also in the galleries are Jana's pottery, collections of historical and contemporary books, drawings, prints, and paintings. Unless otherwise noted, all of the cards and photographs used in this book are from Rick's collection.

Thanks also go to the following members of the Mount Rainier National Park Service (NPS) staff who shared their time, making this a more accurate and enjoyable work: Randy King, park superintendent; Brooke Childrey and the NPS Mount Rainier curatorial staff, for help in finding historical photographs; Kevin Bacher; Paul Kennard; Mason Reed; Stefan Lofgren; Darin Swinney; and any others I may have forgotten.

A true bibliography on Mount Rainier would be many pages long. Arthur Martinson's thesis, "Mountain in the Sky: A History of Mt. Rainier National Park" (Washington State University, 1966) covers the early history and the movement for the formation of a national park. *The Challenge of Rainier* (fourth edition) by Dee Molenaar covers the climbing history of the mountain. For facts, figures, and dates, I have been most dependent upon Bette Filley's *The Big Fact Book about Mount Rainier* (Dunamis House, Issaquah, WA, 1996). This volume has the answer to almost any question about Rainier.

Special thanks go to Amy Kline, my editor at Arcadia Publishing, who put up with my jokes. Heidi Waterhouse was my hand-holder when panic set in. Most especially, I would like to thank my wife, Kathy, who cheerfully heard the stories and drove the thousands of miles as we gathered information for this book.

INTRODUCTION

All national parks are appreciated by the people who live near them, but Mount Rainier National Park has the distinction of being visible to the greatest number of people. On a clear day, over three million residents of the Pacific Northwest can look up and see the gleaming mountain from their yard. At 14,410 feet, it is part of the skyline from Everett to Longview, from Bainbridge Island to Vantage. The towns and cities at its feet must accept a little danger with the beauty, as they are threatened by its active status. It is currently quiet, but long ago, when the Native Americans called it Tahoma, it was more restless. The evidence of lahars and volcanic ash are found in the region's rich farm valleys.

Early European explorers were attracted to the mountain for both adventure and wealth. Those who wanted to climb it hired tribal guides. Bailey Willis was sent by the Northern Pacific Railroad to survey the area for coal deposits. He marked out a trail from Wilkeson to the Mowich River, and then up to the Carbon Glacier. Using the trail established by Willis, George Driver set up a guide service for tourists being ferried up to the mountain by a train from Tacoma.

On the Paradise side, James Longmire spent two decades exploring the Nisqually and Cowlitz Valleys to find a better route between Walla Walla and Olympia. In 1883, he discovered mineral springs, which he developed into a resort in 1884. The resort became a family business, with his wife supervising the girls in the cooking and housekeeping, and the boys serving as coach drivers, road builders, hunters, and guides.

With the construction of a base camp at Longmire Springs, more and more people were willing to undertake the three- to four-day trip from Tacoma to the mountain. As more people came, Longmire was able to further promote visits to the mountain and press for transportation improvements, which in turn allowed more people to come. With the arrival of the Tacoma Eastern Railroad in Ashford in 1904, the trip to and from the mountain could be done in a day, and soon, hundreds of visitors were arriving each day.

By the mid-1890s, the state's population had quadrupled since the 1880 census. Expanding railroads were searching for coal and timber sources. At the same time, the conservation movement, headed by John Muir, Theodore Roosevelt, Gifford Pinchot, George Grinell, and others, was attempting to preserve America's wild and beautiful spaces. There was a surge of national park establishments: Yellowstone in 1872, Sequoia and Kings Canyon in 1890, Yosemite in 1890, and Mount Rainier in 1899.

Although the land had been set aside, Congress did not allocate funds for anything else. When Congress established the Park Service with the National Park Service Organic Act (1916), the stated purpose was "to conserve the scenery and the natural and historic objects and the wild life therein and to provide for the enjoyment of the same in such manner and by such means as will leave them unimpaired for the enjoyment of future generations." Funding for any other development came through investments by concessionaires who created trails, hotels, bridges, and attractions. The concessionaires recouped their investment by attracting tourists willing to pay for their amenities.

Concessions are a license by the NPS for a group or individual to conduct business within the park. The proceeds received by the park are to be used to improve services to park visitors. Over the years, there have been concessions for lodging, transportation, guide services, food service, and boat and ski rental, among many others. The concessionaire negotiates with the Park Service over terms and conditions of the concession, including the price to be paid for the privilege of doing business within the park. In the early years, each park superintendent negotiated concessions.

Stephen T. Mather, the first director of the National Park Service, set about standardizing terms, conditions, and income from concessions in the system's parks. To simplify administration, he sought to have a single all-services concessionaire per park. For Mount Rainier, that would be the Rainier National Park Company of Tacoma. The company's partnership with the Park Service worked well in the early years. As time went on, however, changing circumstances forced the parties apart. The Great Depression reduced the number of visitors and the amount of money those visitors were willing to spend in the park. More often than not, visitors were "day-trippers" who went home and did not stay for the week at an inn or in the cabins. World War II further cut into the number of visitors and caused appropriations and staffing levels to be cut below minimal maintenance levels. After the war, facilities were in terrible shape, Congress was unwilling or unable to fund repairs, visitation soared, and concessionaire investors were concerned that, short of turning national parks into theme parks such as Disneyland, they could not earn a sufficient return on their investment.

Many of the picture postcards of Mount Rainier were produced, sponsored, or influenced by the Rainier National Park Company. A review of available cards shows that most were used as advertisements for the activities of the concessionaire. There are many cards for the Paradise Inn, horseback riding, tours of the ice caves, guided hikes to Eagle and Pinnacle Peaks, bus tours, and views of the mountain on guided walks at Paradise or Sunrise. Missing are views of activities that were not sponsored by the concessionaire. There are few cards of people, events, camping, picnicking, the East Side and Westside Roads, the Wonderland Trail, or the Carbon River–Mowich areas of the park. To fill in these gaps, I have included photographs from the National Park Service–Mount Rainier archives and other services. In 1952, the National Park Service agreed with the Rainier National Park Company that the Park Service would own the structures in the park and the company would provide operations. One effect of this change was that the company's promotion of guest services in the park declined, and with it new postcards.

This book follows a route around Mount Rainier, starting at the Nisqually entrance. Some captions include references to highway milepost markers—readers can use these to compare the historical photographs to the views of today. The references are Nisqually Valley Road (NVR), Westside Road (WR), Paradise Valley Road (PVR), Stevens Canyon Road (SCR), the Eastside Road or State Highway 123 (Hwy 123), the Mather Memorial Highway or State Highway 410 (MMH), the Carbon River Road (CRR), and the Mowich Lake Road or State Highway 165 (MLR). The Wonderland Trail images start at Longmire and circle the mountain in a clockwise route. Day hikes are sorted by their trailheads. A traveler who stops to look at the pictures, however, should be safe and obey all traffic laws.

The story of this national park and its meaning to the surrounding area can be traced through the picture postcards people sent and kept. Mount Rainier is a destination, an aspiration, a reminder that the natural world is still within sight, even when we are creeping along crowded freeways or looking up from our homes in the valleys she oversees.

One

EARLY YEARS ON THE
ROAD TO LONGMIRE

While sailing near the current community of Port Townsend, Capt. George Vancouver of the Royal Navy saw, on May 8, 1792, far to the south, a tall "round snowy mountain." He entered this mountain into his logs and charts as "Mount Rainier," after his friend Rear Adm. Peter Rainier. This sketch is from records of HMS *Discovery* as it sailed south into Puget Sound days later. (Courtesy of NPS Mount Rainier Archives.)

116. Mount Tacoma, from Puyallup River, Tacoma, Wash.

Dr. William Fraser Tolmie was working for the Hudson's Bay Company at Fort Nisqually when, in August 1833, he led an expedition of six men up the Puyallup River to the confluence of the Mowich River, then into the Carbon River Valley. Legend has it that he climbed Tolmie Peak.

In November 1870, the Northern Pacific Railroad completed a spur line from Tacoma, which provided a market for the rich coal deposits in the Carbon River basin. The route allowed visitors to reach the base of the mountains in hours rather than days. Note how steep the canyon walls are. (Courtesy of Historic Carbonado Saloon.)

Bailey Willis, an employee of the Northern Pacific Railroad, explored the area from Wilkeson to the glaciers. He laid out a trail that ran from Wilkeson to the Mowich River and to Spray Park near the foot of the mountain. As a side business, he constructed a small lodge for visitors where the Mowich River joins the Carbon River. This view is of the coal mines and railroad along the Carbon River. (Courtesy of Historic Carbonado Saloon.)

MT. RAINIER FROM SPRAY PARK, RAINIER NATIONAL PARK
REACHED VIA UNION PACIFIC RAILROAD

George Driver started guiding people in 1881 from the Wilkeson train to various sites in the area that was to become the national park. A favorite was the trip to Spray Park and the Carbon Glacier. The term *park*, when used at Rainier, refers to a wet meadow or open space below the glaciers with few if any trees. It is in these parks that the wildflowers grow in abundance.

TACOMA, Wash:
Mount Tacoma, from Tacoma Hotel.

Built in 1884, the five-story Tacoma Hotel marked Tacoma as something more than a raw frontier town. The Northern Pacific Railroad promoted the hotel and excursions to Mount Rainier in national and international publications. One of the favorite excursions was a train trip to Wilkeson, followed by a horseback ride to the foot of the Carbon Glacier.

Tacoma Hotel, Tacoma, Wash.

The architecture of the hotel proved very popular. It was adopted by other buildings of the time in Tacoma, including the city hall, churches, and Stadium High School. The hotel, made of red brick, stucco, and white stone trim, was erected high on a bluff overlooking the harbor. It burned down in 1935.

This early adventurer is taking a photograph of alpine wildflowers with her Folding Pocket Kodak Camera. First introduced in 1898, it is now considered the ancestor of all modern roll-film cameras. It produced a negative two and one-fourth inches by three and one-fourth inches, which remained the standard size for decades. The 3A model, introduced in 1903, had a "Post Card" format of three and one-fourth inches by five and one-half inches, or the 122-film size. The photographer could then directly expose the negative on paper stock sold by the company and send it as a postcard. The 3A camera was sold between 1903 and 1915, with later variations available until 1934. In 1903, a new camera sold for $10.50. Many of the photographs in this book listed as real-photo postcards were taken with a folding pocket camera. (Courtesy of Foothills Historical Society and Museum, Buckley, Washington.)

With the arrival of the Tacoma Eastern Railroad to Ashford in July 1904, the three-day stagecoach ride from Tacoma to Longmire Springs could be accomplished in one morning. There was a daily stage service from Ashford to Longmire Springs. Seen here is an excursion on June 22, 1919, of 125 convalescents from Camp Lewis hospital and 125 girls from Tacoma Catholic churches. (Courtesy of Tacoma Public Library.)

In 1910, Secretary of the Interior Richard A. Ballinger, who was responsible for the operations of the national parks, visited Mount Rainier. He directed then-superintendent Edward Hall to construct an arch to welcome visitors. The work was soon under way, using large cedars from the area. This gateway remained in place until 1972, when it was replaced by a new gate, which continues to welcome visitors

A popular activity over the years has been to take a picture of the gateway to show the folks back home that the visitor actually made it. In this c. 1920 photograph, three motor coaches are seen coming down from Longmire Springs, probably on their daily trip to the train depot in Ashford.

There are two historic buildings at the Nisqually entrance. The Oscar Brown cabin, not visible here, is out of frame to the right and was built in 1908 to serve the seasonal rangers who rode horses on a circuit to protect the park and its resources. Also unseen in this view, to the left on a small knoll, is the superintendent's house that was built in 1915. (Courtesy of NPS Rainier Archives.)

One of the first things visitors saw after passing through the Nisqually entrance was the Sunshine Point Campground. This year-round campground, available for tent camping, was built by the Civilian Conservation Corps as a Depression-era work opportunity for young men. From 1933 to 1940, over 1,000 men came annually to Rainier to work on infrastructure in the park. The campground was destroyed by floods in 2006. (Courtesy of NPS Mount Rainier Information.)

During the eight years of operation, there were over 25 camps established in the park. The CCC built campgrounds, improved trails, erected the famed arch entryways, and provided wildfire protection. Sunshine Point Campground was the site of the first year-round CCC camp, in 1937, and was one of the last to close, in 1940. (Courtesy of NPS Mount Rainier Archives.)

The turn for the Westside Road is nine-tenths of a mile from the Nisqually entrance. As of 2012, the road is opened to Fish Creek, which is three miles from the junction. A road circling the mountain was nothing less than a dream. Survey work was started in 1913, and in 1924 funding became available for work to start northward from the Nisqually Road and southward from the Carbon River Valley. This view is of the Tahoma Glacier.

The Borden family were early homesteaders living near the Nisqually River in Ashford. Like many families in the area, they had various sources of income, including farming, logging, renting packhorses to the guides, and working in the park's hotels. Here, Ruth Borden (seated on the right) and members of her family explore the new Westside Road. (Courtesy of Marie Fore.)

17

On December 10, 1946, a Marine Corps R5C transport plane was headed from San Diego to Seattle with 32 aboard. Strong winds blew the plane many miles off course. The pilot was authorized to rise above the clouds. Before it could gain elevation, however, the plane hit the South Tahoma Glacier near the 9,000-foot level, killing all aboard. A memorial was placed at Round Point on the Westside Road. (Courtesy of NPS Mount Rainier Archives.)

This late-1920s image shows one of the bridges on the Westside Road crossing St. Andrews Creek. The road was not completed due to a combination of rough terrain, "rotten rock," and lack of funds. Flooding near Tahoma Creek has closed the road to vehicles for the foreseeable future. (Courtesy of NPS Mount Rainier Archives.)

The Mowich and Westside Roads were to meet on the ridge, as seen here from the Kapowsin Tree Plantation. Also visible is one of the mountain's lenticular (lens-shaped) clouds, or cloud cap. These clouds are formed when moisture-laden wind currents are disturbed as they pass over the mountain. Such clouds often forecast rain.

Horse-drawn stages or coaches were used to transport visitors from Tacoma Eastern Depot in Ashford to the hotels at Longmire Springs. The "U.S. Government Road" on the label of this postcard was a replacement for the local county road. This road was designed and built by the Army Corps of Engineers to carry the heavy coaches and wagons making the trip between Longmire Springs and Ashford. This card was mailed in 1909.

Tahoma Creek in years past offered visitors the first view of the mountain once they were in the park. Trees have since grown to block much of the view. The creek is the drainage for the Tahoma Glacier. Outflows from the Tahoma Glacier have buried trees trunks many feet deep in debris. If the trees die, there may be a new "silver forest" and perhaps a new view of the mountain. The creek is to the lower left.

The next creek crossing is named for
Lt. August Valentine Kautz, who, in
1857, made a nearly successful summit.
He and a party of four from Fort
Steilacoom followed a route up the
Nisqually River, around the terminus
of the Nisqually Glacier to Van Trump
Park, then up and across the glacier that
now bears his name. Looking up the
creek, today's travelers may be able to
see the glacier.

Kautz Creek offered a demonstration of
the force of glaciers. In October 1947,
a mudflow exploded out of the snout
of the glacier. In less than 15 hours,
an estimated 50 million cubic yards of
debris moved down to Alder Lake. The
silt reduced the capacity of the reservoir
by a third. The forest of dead trees
shown here is caused by rocks and other
debris stripping the trees of their bark
and burying the roots under feet of silt.
(NVR milepost 3.2.)

Mt. Rainier from Kautz Fork
Rainier National Park   2530

The unidentified couple in this 1905 real-photo postcard is crossing one of the early bridges on the Government Road between the Nisqually entrance and Longmire Springs. In winter, the heavy wagons turned the road into a 10-mile mud pit. Disputes over right-of-way and design standards delayed construction of this much-needed link. (Courtesy of Marie Fore.)

Giant Firs seen after entering Rainier National Park, Wn

It was difficult for the park to secure adequate financing during the early years. One way to save money on road construction was to build the road around trees, rather than to clear a right-of-way. Early visitors to the park were impressed with the sizes of the trees and the thickness of the forest. There was little in the East or Europe that could match these old-growth conifer forests.

Two

Longmire and Upriver

James Longmire of Newton, Indiana, was an early pioneer to Western Washington. In 1853, he was part of the first wagon train that crossed the Naches Trail from Walla Walla to the area now known as Yelm. This trip passed close to Mount Rainier. Starting the next summer, he commenced 30 years of exploring the west, south, and east slopes of the mountain. By 1870, he was acknowledged as the best guide and outfitter for others seeking to get a closer view of the mountain. It was in these roles that he guided Stevens and Van Trump on the first recorded successful ascent of Mount Rainier. Joining Van Trump and George Bayley on the third ascent when he was 65, Longmire discovered the mineral hot springs that were named for him. (Courtesy of NPS Mount Rainier Archives.)

Morning at Longmires Springs, Mt. Rainier.

The first Longmire Hotel was built in 1884. It had accommodations for five guests and the Longmire family. It proved popular and was expanded to a larger hotel in 1890, seen here. The Longmire Hotel burned down in 1910, by which time newer and larger hotels served the area. (Courtesy of Linda Lewis.)

The Trail of the Shadows is an easy 0.7-mile-long loop across the road from the present inn. It allows visitors to see the original Longmire spread where the hotel, cabins, pond, and springs were located. Parts of the wall in this c. 1905 photograph can still be seen by walkers. (NVR milepost 6.2.)

Between 1905 and 1916, as many as seven hotels housed visitors in the Longmire Springs area. Some of the hotels were little more than tents, and others were more luxurious. In 1916, the majority of commercial activities in the park were consolidated into the Rainier National Park Company. This appears to be the National Park Inn Annex, which was rotated and moved after the first National Park Inn burned. This side of the building now faces the mountain.

The Tacoma Eastern Railroad built this, their first hotel at Longmire Springs, in 1906. They then set about promoting the hotel and line across the country. The railroad provided excursion services for groups, with over 100 mountain climbers arriving at a time. A second edition of the National Park Inn in Longmire was opened to the public in 1918 after two years of construction.

Visitors were impressed with the National Park Inn's massive rustic interior furnishings; crafted by Swiss–German Hans Grussion, they were built to resemble those of European hunting lodges. Grussion used cedar logs that he recovered from a nearby burn as his raw material. This postcard shows the exterior, sitting room, dining room, and lobby. The inn burned down in 1922. (Courtesy of Linda Lewis.)

This real-photo postcard shows the motor coaches used at Longmire Springs around 1916. These were likely the coaches operated by the Tacoma Carriage & Baggage Company. The company transported visitors to and from the depot in Ashford and up the mountain to Paradise Park and Valley. (Courtesy of South Pierce County Historical Society.)

Proposed Hotel at Longmire Springs, Mount Rainier.

During the first half of the 20th century, as now, the Park Service was responsible for protecting the wildlife, environment, and infrastructure. Concessionaires provided visitors with food, lodging, and activities. Concessionaires paid the Park Service according to a contract, hoping they could make a profit. They were constantly looking for ways to increase the revenues they could generate from the visitors. At Mount Rainier, the number of day-visitors was much higher and per-visitor incomes lower than at other western national parks. This view is a concept design from a concessionaire for the development of Longmire intended to draw more visitors. It appears very similar to the plan for the 1909 Alaska-Yukon Exhibition in Seattle. This plan called for a major hotel in the center, a concert hall, a shopping concourse, and formal gardens. The National Park Service declined the proposal.

These later-model motor coaches were used to transport visitors to and from the train depot in Ashford or up the mountain to Paradise. In the background is the National Park Inn Annex. Promotion of the park by the Tacoma Eastern Railroad kept all of the hotels full during the July–October "season."

In this 1931 view of the Longmire Plaza, the administration building is to the left, and the first museum is in the center. The gas station and National Park Inn are out of the frame to the right of this image. The plaza pictured here is much larger than the present-day plaza; the plan for Longmire called for more green and less asphalt. Revegetation projects have returned the area to a more natural setting. (Courtesy of NPS Rainier Archives.)

This c. 1917 photograph of the mountain from Longmire Springs shows cars parking on the meadow. From Longmire, hikers could travel to Eagle Peak, Rampart Ridge, Van Trump Park, and points along the Wonderland Trail. This view also shows how popular automobiles were in the park's early years. In many ways, the park was designed to accommodate automobiles. (Courtesy of NPS Rainier Archives.)

The gas station at Longmire, pictured here in the early 1950s, was opened in 1929 by the Standard Oil Company. It was the first service station constructed in a national park. In addition to gas, the station provided tires and light mechanical repairs. The gas station now is an interpretive center focusing on the role of transportation in the park. (Courtesy of NPS Rainier Archives.)

The second administration building was constructed in 1928 in the National Park rustic style. The original administrative center opened in 1916 and became a museum and visitor center. The ground floor of this building now provides hikers with information and backcountry permits. (NVR milepost 6.3) (Courtesy of National Park Service Rainier Archives.)

Over the years, additional buildings have been constructed at Longmire to support the operation of the park. This residence was built to meet the housing needs of rangers and other year-round Park Service employees. (Courtesy of National Park Service Rainier Archives.)

ALASKA DOG TEAM at NISQUALLY BRIDGE, Rainier National Park

The suspension bridge across the Nisqually River connects the Nisqually Road with a wagon road and Native American trails that James Longmire used to connect the springs area with the Bear Prairie–Skate Creek route. The Longmire campground and community building are across the river from the Longmire village. The sled dogs were among the winter activities the concessionaire used to promote winter use of the National Park Inn.

The community building at Longmire is located across the river, near the area of the former Longmire Campground. Built in 1927, it has been used in many different ways. In this building, rangers often presented evening programs to campers staying in the campground. (Courtesy of National Park Service Rainier Archives.)

In recent years, the Community Building has continued to serve the public. It has been used as a conference center, employee training facility, a press center, and a weather-safe wedding chapel within the park. (Courtesy of National Park Service Rainier Archives.)

The campground at Longmire opened in 1918. During the Depression, much was done to improve the facilities at the campgrounds. This photograph from the early 1960s shows tables, fire pits, running water, and flush toilets built by the CCC or WPA. The campgrounds closed as the new Cougar Rock facility opened. Today, the old campground is used as temporary housing for park volunteers. (Courtesy of National Park Service Rainier Archives.)

The motor coaches seen in this c. 1917 postcard are continuing up the road past Longmire to Paradise. The Mountain Highway in the park was built in bits and pieces. In 1903, famed civil engineer Eugene Ricksecker undertook a survey to establish a road from the Nisqually entrance to Paradise Valley. (NVR milepost 6.4.)

These visitors enjoy the roar of a river around 1905. The women are well protected from the elements with heavy clothing and wide-brimmed hats. Contrary to the card notation, this is not the Nisqually River. This river is very narrow, and there are few signs of past flooding. The best guess is that this is the Paradise River. (Courtesy of Jim Hale.)

Most of the creeks and rivers in the park are described as "braided," or having a channel that consists of a network of smaller channels separated by small and often temporary islands called braid bars. The rivers run through debris left behind by retreating glaciers. Care should be taken in streambeds, as the rocks are unstable. In high water, the rocks can be heard tumbling. This is a real-photo postcard.

The Nisqually Road crosses the Van Trump Creek at Christine Falls. The proximity of the falls to the highway is one of the encounters with nature that visitors experience in the park. This first bridge across the creek was built by the Army Corps of Engineers in 1902. (Courtesy of NPS Rainier Archives.)

This, the second road bridge across the Van Trump Creek, was completed in the late 1920s. This is in the National Park rustic style that was later adopted by the CCC. There is a short trail on the downhill side of the road that allows access to the creek.

The Rainier National Park Company was formed in 1916. In the years following, it invested in many projects to improve visitor services and reduce cost. This hydroelectric power plant was located on Van Trump Creek, some two miles up the Nisqually River from Longmire. Built in 1916 to provide electricity to Longmire, the 420-foot head (fall of water) produced over 250 horsepower at peak power, and the project cost $11,000. (NVR milepost 10.5) (Courtesy of NPS Rainier Archives.)

Nisqually Glacier at Mt. Rainier, Seattle, Wash.

ICE CAVES, NISQUALLY GLACIER,

RAINIER NATIONAL PARK, WASHINGTON

By 1910, a motor road was opened to the public as far as the Nisqually River and glacier. The bridge across the river and the grade up to Ricksecker Point posed significant construction challenges. The first car reached Paradise in 1911, and the road was opened to the public in 1915. These mountaineers (note alpenstocks) have climbed to the face of the Nisqually glacier. (NVP milepost 11.5.)

When the road to Paradise was laid out in 1903, the terminus of the Nisqually Glacier was just a few hundred feet from the proposed road. This party is exploring the ice caves at the "snout" of the glacier. By the 1930s, the glacier was retreating up the valley, leaving behind a moraine of loose broken rock.

36

Looking up to Glacier, Source of Nisqually River, Western Washington

Here is a clear view of the terminus of the glacier. Over the years, the glaciers grow and recede. In 1840, the terminus was several hundred yards below the current Nisqually bridge. In 1956, the terminus was at a record high elevation. The US Geological Survey (USGS) keeps detailed records of the glaciers. In the early second decade of the 21st century, the trend is clearly for receding glaciers.

In this August 1955 real-photo postcard, the glacier had retreated to some 3,000 feet above the bridge. This is close to the documented record of 1955 and puts it out of view around on the back side of Van Trump Park. (Courtesy of Marie Fore.)

This real-photo postcard was sent in 1918. The travelers are posing in front of the Nisqually Glacier at the bottom of the Canyon Rim Grade. In the background can be seen the "snout" of the glacier and, above that, more of the glacier. The mountain is at the top. There is snow on the side hill, indicating that this scene took place in late spring or early summer.

The Canyon Rim Grade, the stretch of road from the Nisqually River to Ricksecker Point, was one of the most difficult to construct. The current driving surface is the result of nearly 30 years of effort. The Canyon Rim viewpoint allows the visitor to get a clear view of the mountain and of thousands of acres of old-growth forest.

Nisqually Glacier, Mt. Tacoma, Wash.

A caravan of Buick cars undertakes an expedition to Paradise around 1916. Buick dealers were noted at the time for organizing such events. Note the width of the roadway. At this stretch of the road, many early automobiles had problems with overheating, tire damage, and other mechanical problems. The glacier is the dark space at left center. (Courtesy of Marie Fore.)

RAINIER NATIONAL PARK

1656   HIGHWAY AT RICKSECKER POINT

Ricksecker Point has spectacular views of Mount Rainier, the Tatoosh Range, and the upper Nisqually River. The Canyon Rim Grade was very hard for horses drawing wagons and for early cars. The viewpoint provided water for overheated horses and radiators. From 1908 to 1924, the grade was open only to one-way traffic; rangers held traffic at the Nisqually Bridge for uphill traffic and at the vista point for downhill travel. Ricksecker Point was named for Eugene Ricksecker, a civilian engineer who was hired by the US Army Corps of Engineers to build the road from Longmire Springs to Paradise Park and Valley. Ricksecker was a pioneer in highway engineering. The road he surveyed and then constructed implemented the highest engineering and safety standards of his day while maintaining the natural aesthetics of the park. Ricksecker's beliefs about vistas are also apparent in the design of the Blue Ridge Parkway and other sweeping national park views. (NVP milepost 12.5.)

Narada Falls on the Paradise River drops 168 feet into Paradise Valley. The falls were named by a small group of Theosophists in reference to a spiritual being worshipped by the Brahman people of India, *Narada* meaning "uncontaminated." There are several viewpoints beside the falls and trails that go to Reflection Lakes and Cougar Rock. (NVR milepost 14.5.)

The original road to Paradise Park crossed the Paradise River at Narada Falls, turned to the right, then used several switchbacks to reach Inspiration Point. Here can be seen one of the switchbacks across the valley from the current road. For many years, this was a one-way road.

SWITCHBACKS ON ROAD TO PARADISE INN, RAINIER NATIONAL PARK.

As the road climbed the steep grade from Narada Falls, it crossed the river several times, including a series of seven cascades called the Seven Sisters. For many years, this was a one-way stretch of road, and cars were held at Narada Falls Viewpoint to wait their turn to enter Paradise.

This view of the Seven Sisters was mailed from Elma Washington on February 29, 1908. The format of the card is one of the oldest styles in the collection. After the photograph was taken, it was then sent to Germany, where color was added and the card printed. Finally, it was sent back to the United States to be sold in the park.

Pres. William Howard Taft visited the park in October 1911. A longtime friend of Theodore Roosevelt, he was interested in conservation efforts and controls on corporations. The plan was for the president to drive to Paradise. Ongoing road construction and recent rains made the road above Longmire Springs a river of mud, and the party did not reach Paradise. (Courtesy of NPS Rainier Archives.)

MOUNTAIN AND HIGHWAY AT INSPIRATION POINT

Inspiration Point was where the Nisqually Valley Road reached the ridge before entering Paradise Valley. With the construction of the Stevens Canyon Road and the need to add fill to widen the new road, much of the old road disappeared. Note the width of the road. When the road was one-way, cars waited their turn at Inspiration Point. (SCR milepost .3)

Three

PARADISE

This view of Paradise is from the 1960s. The road, beginning in the lower left, passes the site of the campground on the left, the housekeeping cabins to the left and right, and then the picnic grounds to the right. The Jackson Visitor Center is the round building in the lower center. The Paradise Inn and Guide House are the next group of buildings, in the upper right. The Paradise Valley Road curves to the right.

Camp of the Clouds was first established in 1886 at the 5,900-foot level on the east end of Alta Vista Ridge. The tent hotel was set up and removed each year. It offered a spectacular view of both the mountain and the Tatoosh Ridge, as seen in this real-photo postcard.

John Reese of Ashford took over the operation of Camp of the Clouds and combined it with his own High View Camp. His operations were the only public accommodations in the Paradise Valley prior to 1916. One of the unfortunate legacies of these early camps is the damage done to the subalpine meadows. A hundred years later, work continues to repair the damage with revegetation projects.

The staff members of the Camp of the Clouds in 1911 were mostly from the Ashford area. In this real-photo postcard, Kate Borden, standing in the middle, is surrounded by family members and neighbors. The camp was open from mid-July to the end of September. This is just one of the several income-generating projects the Borden family undertook each year. (Courtesy of Marie Fore.)

Paradise Valley was popular with many early movie crews. With easy rail transportation from California and the East and the guarantee of snow eight months out of the year, it was often used as a winter location. It is hard to tell if the crew in this real-photo postcard was actually filming or just having a good time. (Courtesy of Marie Fore.)

July Snowballing in Paradise Valley. Rainier National Park. 2551

Visitors were often surprised to discover snow many feet deep late into July. Here, a group of visitors are enjoying summertime in the snow. The mountain is looming in the background. The first snowfall of the new season could be expected sometime after the middle of October.

The National Park Service was created by Congress in 1916. In subsequent reorganization, the concessionaires were consolidated into one per park. The Rainier National Park Company had professional management and was better capitalized than the smaller organizations. Crews were brought from all over the Northwest to help build the Paradise Inn, housed in this temporary camp. The building had to be framed, roofed, and sealed in a single construction season. This is a real-photo postcard. (Courtesy of Marie Fore.)

The Paradise Inn opened with a public celebration on Sunday, July 1, 1917. The inn had 129 rooms ready for use, and tents were set up to house overflow guests until an additional 100 rooms were completed in 1920. Many locals from the Upper Nisqually Valley worked to get the inn ready on time.

This real-photo postcard depicts the Paradise parking lot. According to notes in the family album, this photograph was taken by a member of the construction crew following the opening day celebrations. Local legend has it that many families made a special effort to join the celebration.

The main lobby is 50 feet by 112 feet and has two large fireplaces—one at each end—with one chimney over 40 feet tall. A scattering of chairs, tables, and displays provide comfort for visitors. The lobby was a refuge for many when the fog or snow made travel difficult. Evening programs continue to be presented by park rangers or inn staff.

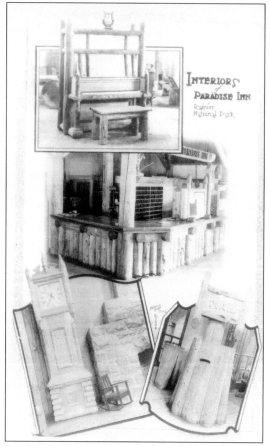

The interior furnishings were hand-crafted by regional artisan Hans Fraehnke. The fabled German craftsman hand-built many of the odd wood creations located throughout the great room. Some of his notable creations are the front desk, grandfather clock, the outgoing mailbox, and the piano, which was played by professionals and amateurs.

CORNER OF THE LOBBY, PARADISE INN, RAINIER NATIONAL PARK.

In this c. 1925 postcard, inn visitors are enjoying the unusual lobby furnishings, which were made from locally grown Alaskan cedar recovered from a burned area between Paradise and Longmire. Pres. Harry S Truman made a surprise visit to the mountain in June 1945. Local legend has it that the president enjoyed playing the lobby piano.

Paradise Inn Dining Room

The formal dining room at the Paradise Inn was famed for the quality and heartiness of the meals. It had a professionally trained chef, and word is that the sack lunches prepared for guests going hiking or horseback riding for the day were something special.

In the evening, inn guests could gather around the warmth of the fireplaces. Note the case clock on the left and the photograph of people "nature coasting" to the right of the fireplace. In the fireplace, you can see trees that are part of the fire grate. On the table is a Pacific Northwest Native American basket.

This view of the inn, from the south looking north, was taken before 1922. The inn is finished, but the annex has yet to be started. The annex was opened for the 1922 season. Alta Vista is on the ridge, and the wildflowers are in bloom in the foreground. (PVR milepost .01.)

T-17   PARADISE INN, ELEVATION 5,557 FEET   5A-H566

By the early 1930s, the inn had acquired a more finished look. The completed annex can be seen on the right. The landscaping and paved walkways surrounding the building are complete. Touring cars are ready to load visitors for their adventures or journeys home.

In the mid-1950s, the inn continued to serve as the center for tourists visiting the Paradise area. The parking lot has been expanded to accommodate larger buses and more cars. Buses would take travelers to Sunrise, Stevens Canyon, and some trailheads. There was also scheduled service to Seattle and Tacoma.

51

Deep in winter, the inn is almost completely buried by snow. Paradise is traditionally one of the snowiest places in the world. The 1940–1941 snow season saw 313 inches (26 feet, 1 inch) of snowfall. During the 1971–1972 season, snowfall was measured at 1,122 inches (93 feet, 6 inches).

It is hard to tell what these people are doing on the roof of the inn in the early 1920s. Some have tools, and there are snowshoes in the lower center. It is possible they are removing snow to reduce the weight, because when the snow melts in the spring rains, it gains weight. This is a practice still followed in the area.

27-119   SPRING OPENING, PARADISE INN   A-H568

Crews can be seen digging out the inn in the spring, getting it ready for visitors. The roof has been cleared, and snowplows have cleared the access road. Work is under way to reach the south porch and the main entrance.

Guests arriving at the inn get their first view of the mountain and are startled by the amount of snow. Early in the season, snow lingers at the 5,000-feet elevation through July. To gain access to the lobby, guests need to pass through a tunnel in the drifted snow.

PARADISE LODGE

The Paradise Lodge was opened in 1931 to serve the needs of the growing number of day visitors and those staying at the campground. The lodge had a restaurant, public space, a small store, comfort stations, and, in clear weather, spectacular views of the mountain. The Tatoosh Range can be seen in the background. The lodge was removed to make way for the Jackson Visitor Center.

THE TATOOSH RANGE FROM PARADISE VALLEY, RAINIER NATIONAL PARK, WASHINGTON

The lodge (on the right) and community building (in the center) provided services to day visitors, campers, and those staying in the housekeeping cabins. In poor weather, the community building housed ranger talks and other events. These two buildings were located, along with the curio shop, very near to where the Henry M. Jackson Visitor Center was eventually located.

31-1621 THE MOUNTAIN FROM PARADISE LODGE 6A-H582

The Paradise Lodge provided great views of the mountain and Tatoosh Range and gave easy access to the western end of the Paradise trail system. Parking for the lodge expanded over the years to accommodate the growing number of visitors.

The Paradise Lodge operated for a longer season than did the inn. It remained open in the fall as long as the road was open, sometimes as late as Thanksgiving. In some years, it would open in early May for Mother's Day. The lodge was removed in June 1965 to make room for the new visitor center.

Paradise Visitors Center and Mount Rainier, Washington

In September 1966, a new visitor center opened that was later renamed for Sen. Henry M. Jackson. The center was designed for day visitors and had a gift shop, cafeteria, bookstore, exhibit space, theater, and a 360-degree viewing space. The architecture was not the traditional National Park Rustic, and many felt it looked out of place, but the view from the observation level was spectacular. (NVR milepost 17.2.)

A park ranger points out information on the Paradise area on one of the 3-D models of the park to some young visitors. The interior of the visitor center features ski gear lighting fixtures and interior rockwork. The building had a heated roof system to deal with the heavy snowfall. Over time, this system became very expensive to maintain and operate. (Courtesy of Kevin Bacher.)

The new Henry M. Jackson Visitor Center opened in 2009. It is architecturally in the "Cascadia" style, which is close to other grand National Park Rustic buildings but is adapted to the heavy snowfall. The steep pitch of the roof and massive snow shutters are intended to allow the building to survive the severest winter storm with a minimum of maintenance. (NVP milepost 17.4.) (Courtesy of Kevin Bacher.)

The interior of the new visitor center is very open and spacious. On the ground floor are the information desk, theater, dining area, sitting area, and restrooms. The second floor has interpretive displays, viewing of Mount Rainier and the Tatoosh Ridge, and a gift shop. In winter, with the snow shutters closed, the center feels snug. (Courtesy of Kevin Bacher.)

CROSSING MAZAMA RIDGE ON SKYLINE TRAIL

Horseback riding was a popular activity in the early years at Paradise and was heavily promoted by the Rainier National Park Company. There were several different rides available. Postcards show horses on the Skyline, Lakes, Paradise River, and Pinnacle Peak trails. Ride options included an hour, half a day, a full day, or overnight.

The Skyline Trail was a popular horse ride in the 1920s and 1930s. This is the hitching post, located up-slope from Guide Hut, across the drive from the inn's entrance. Today, the Skyline is a favorite for photographers and those who enjoy the wildflowers.

28-934   On Paradise Glacier   1093-29-N

The first guided tours of the Paradise Ice Caves took place in 1908. The caves were at the terminus of the Paradise Glacier above Paradise. The early tours included crossing glacier snowfields on the way to the cave entrances. Visitors were given instructions on roping-up, use of their alpenstocks, and the proper means to cross a crevasse. Sunlight filtered by the ice created a blue hue.

The caves were subject to scientific study. At times, scientists were able to document an extensive system of caverns. The size of the caverns grew or declined based on how the glacier's movement and the terrain. The Paradise River drains the caves, and several people have been injured or killed when they failed to give the river sufficient respect. These dangers forced the Park Service to limit access to the area.

The caves are formed by air currents and ground warming that melt the glaciers from the bottom up, forming a gap between the ground and the glacier ice. Holes appear where the ice has been thinned by cracking and other movements. Variations in the thickness of the ice change the filtration of sunlight, creating a wide spectrum of blue shades within the caves.

PARADISE ICE CAVE
Mt. Rainier, Washington

As the glacier retreated (melted), its terminus moved uphill and thinned, becoming very unstable. The Paradise Ice Caves were closed to the public in 1971. By 1992, the glacier had retreated to such an extent that the ice caves ceased to exist. Even now, some 40 years after the glaciers were closed, visitors who were privileged to see the caves remember them as something special.

In the early 1920s, the Rainier National Park Company experimented with several unusual visitor services that they hoped would be profitable. One of these was a nine-hole golf course located in Paradise Valley. The tee for the first hole was near the inn, and the green for the ninth was near the picnic area. A bus would bring the golfers back to the inn at the end of their round. (Courtesy of NPS Rainier Archives.)

The golf course was not a success. Few golfers played the course, and the valley was not well suited for the sport. The park company and the Park Service disagreed on how much wildflower acreage should be replaced with tees and greens. It was also soon observed that much of the valley floor is wetland, if not swamp. The course was abandoned after two years. (Courtesy of NPS Rainier Archives.)

Martin Johnson
Custom Photographer

The Paradise Campground had a spectacular view. The mountain framed one end of the camp, and the Tatoosh Range the other. In this photograph from the early 1960s, note the number of RVs. The campground was closed as part of the Mission '66 program, as the area was ill suited for camping. Lack of water, cool and cold nighttime temperatures, thick fogs, and a lack of space for camping trailers all encouraged the Park Service to find a more suitable camping area, which ended up being Cougar Rock. A successful revegetation effort has made the site of the former campground hard to locate.

As soon as the road to Paradise was opened to the public in 1908, camping on the subalpine meadows increased. Some camping practices of the time, such as digging trenches below the walls of tents and starting fires directly on the heather, were very destructive of the meadows. Even 100 years later, a trained observer can spot campsites, toilets, and informal roads and trails.

A SECTION OF PARADISE VALLEY CAMP GROUND, TATOOSH RANGE IN BACKGROUND, Rainier National Park

The Paradise Campground is seen here around 1927. The park was one of the early hosts to the Civilian Conservation Corps (CCC), which arrived in 1933. High on the CCC's "to do" list were improvements to the park's camp and picnic grounds. CCC boys from New York City built rock fireplaces, tables, shelters, restrooms, water and septic systems, and laid out roads.

30.2262   HOUSEKEEPING CABINS AT PARADISE   1A290

The Rainier National Park Company introduced housekeeping cabins, opening 275 cabins at Paradise in 1931. The Great Depression was hard on the company. At the outbreak of World War II, the company sold the cabins to defense contractors in the Puget Sound area at more than cost. The infusion of income helped the company survive the war.

30.2180   HOUSEKEEPING CABINS AT PARADISE   1A287

The cabins were located in a meadow that extended from what is now the parking for the odl Jackson Visitor Center to the west end of the current picnic area. Each cabin had a kitchen/ living room area and separate sleeping areas. Similar cabins appeared at many other national parks at about the same time.

Mount Rainier appears at one end of Paradise. On the other end is the Tatoosh Range, which runs east to west as seen from the Paradise area. Stevens Peak (at 6,510 feet) is in the east. Pinnacle Peak, near the center, is reached by a one-and-a-half-mile hike from the Reflection Lakes parking area. This view is from near Alta Vista.

Paradise Inn in Mid-Winter

Eagle Peak, with an elevation of 5,954 feet, is the west end of the ridge (the tall peak on the right). It is reached by a 3.5-mile trail that starts near the Community Building at Longmire. The trail ends at a saddle with a great view. Special skills are needed to climb the peak. This view is from above the inn in late winter.

Most of the downhill skiers have left the mountain to pursue their sport at more developed sites. That has left Paradise to sled riders, cross-country skiers, and snowshoers. A sledding hill near the visitor center is monitored by rangers and is open when there is sufficient snow, about five feet. Rangers also lead snowshoe tours, and snowshoes may be rented at the visitor center gift shop.

Skiers have long enjoyed the quiet beauty of the mountain. Paradise can now be reached most days during the winter. Crews try to keep the road from Longmire open, but severe storms may close it for a few days at a time. Posts 10 feet in height serve to mark the edge of the roads for snowplows. Guest services during the winter months are limited to holidays and weekends.

36-101 Open Terrain near the Mountain in Spring
...ainier Nat'l. Park

Many people think that Mount Rainier is most beautiful in summer, when it exhibits all of the wildflowers. But they may have never seen the mountain in her winter gowns. With 10 or 20 feet of snow, the mountain's rough edges are gone and any rocky scars are smoothed away. Many visitors enjoy putting on cross-country skis or snowshoes and following the trails above Paradise. The sled run near the visitor center is popular with families. Visiting the mountain in winter requires additional precautions, and visitors should be familiar with special park requirements during that time. Additional information can be obtained by visiting the park's website at www.nps.gov/mora.

The caption on the back of this mid-1930s postcard reads, "Rainier National Park is unexcelled for its ski terrain. Unlimited, unobstructed ski runs over deep snow, on the south side of Mount Rainier, thrill thousands of ardent sports fans each year." Many regional residents were Scandinavian immigrants, and they helped promote the sport.

From 1933 to 1940, the Silver Ski Championship, a downhill race, was held annually. The course started at Camp Muir (10,000 feet) and ended near the Paradise Inn (5,500 feet). The race was for professional skiers from the Western United States and Canada. The first racer to complete the course was named the winner. This was later changed to the skier with the best time. In 1934, the winner completed the four-and-a-half-mile course in seven and a half minutes.

36-117   *Ski Action in Mount Rainier National Park*

SKI MEET AT MT. RAINIER, WASHINGTON—P86

Since the early 1920s, a spring snow festival has been held. First centered around Longmire, it later moved to Paradise and the Paradise Inn. In some years, it was held in conjunction with the ski championship, and in other years, as a separate event. In this photograph, it appears to have been held later in the year, as the snow has melted around the inn. (Courtesy of Mineral Lake Lodge.)

The dogsled rides started at Longmire around 1920 and then were moved to Paradise. The business was never very profitable. In the days before meal-based dog food, the sled dogs ate a lot of fish and meat. Fish were cheap in Alaska, but that was not the case on the mountain. And during the summer season, there was neither snow nor business.

During World War II, Mount Rainier joined the war effort, serving as an Alpine and winter training center for some of the troops stationed at Fort Lewis. The 10th Mountain Division made extensive use of the mountain for testing equipment, teaching arctic and winter skills, and learning how to use equipment in very cold temperatures. Other troops used the mountain to learn how to use and spot snow camouflage.

The first recorded skiing in the park was in 1912. With the introduction of a towrope in the early 1930s, skiers were pulled up the hill, and decades of contention began. The concessionaire and skiers wanted more and bigger lifts, but the Park Service and other visitors wanted to prohibit the introduction of permanent structures on the alpine meadows and above. The last year for the ski towropes at Paradise was 1973.

Skiing on Mazama Ridge, Rainier National Park, Washington

RAINIER NATIONAL PARK

T-87   HIGHWAY ENTERING PARADISE VALLEY

The ridge to the east of Paradise rising over the Paradise Valley is called Mazama, which is an indigenous word from a now unknown language for "mountain goat" and the name of a famed Portland climbing club. To reach this spot, the skiers could have taken the towrope, then followed the Lakes Trail and then the ridge line. They could return to the lodge using the access road or the valley floor.

Until 1923, the Paradise Valley Road was the only road to the Paradise Park. The road follows the Paradise Valley from Narada Falls, crossing the river several times until it reaches Inspiration Point. From there, it skirts the lower levels of the Mazama Ridge along the east side of Paradise Valley. It enters Paradise Park near the inn.

Four

STEVENS CANYON AND EAST AND NORTH SIDES

This photograph of the Stevens Canyon Road was taken in 1964 from near Faraway Rock on the Upper Lakes Trail. Stevens Peak is overlooking the valley. The canyon is named for Hazard Stevens, an Army officer and one of the first to summit. His father was the first governor of Washington Territory. The ridgetop is near 5,600 feet.

Mt. Reflected in Reflection Lake - Rainier Nat'l Pk

The view of the mountain from Reflection Lake is a favorite for visitors and puzzle makers alike. There is an easy trail around the lake, but it is muddy early in the season. Bugs also enjoy the lake, and the visitor should be prepared. One of the earliest trails from Paradise was the Lower Lakes Trail, which brought visitors to Reflection Lake and her smaller sister, Louise Lake, from the lodge. The Upper Lakes Trail goes from the east end of the lakes to the inn. The Wonderland Trail passes by the lakes as it comes up from Stevens Canyon and before dropping down to Narada Falls. Across the road from the lake, trailheads led to Pinnacle Peak and Snow Lake. The early road builders also provided access to the lakes from Inspiration Point. (SCR milepost 1.1)

In 1927, the Mount Rainier Company sought to capitalize on the popularity of Reflection Lake with a boat rental and general store concession. Swimmers have found the lake to be very cold. Unfortunately, ripples from the boats spoiled the reflection of the mountain. Visitors complained, and soon, the lake was free of boats. Swimming in the lake is now prohibited to protect the fragile lakeshore.

Stevens Ridge is on the north side of Stevens Canyon, which flows from the northwest to the southeast. The ridgetop is near 5,600 feet, some 2,000 feet higher than the road, which is about 1,000 feet higher than the river.

Stevens Peak is on the east end of the Tatoosh Ridge and forms the south ridge of Stevens Canyon. In this view, Unicorn Peak is to the right. This view is from somewhere between Paradise and Camp Muir.

At Box Canyon, there is an interpretive display on glaciers. The trail from the parking lot, along the fence line, takes the visitor to an overview of the Muddy Fork of the Cowlitz River. This deep canyon was marked in part by glacial striation and demonstrates how the park is constantly changing. (SCR milepost 8.5) (Courtesy of NPS Rainier Archives.)

The Grove of the Patriarchs is a collection of ancient and large old-growth Douglas fir, western red cedar, and western hemlock trees growing along the eastern bank of the Ohanapecosh River. In this photograph, a visitor is examining one of the cedars. The grove is reached by an easy mile-and-a-half, round-trip trail. Along the trail are informative signs identifying plants and points of interest. There is a swing bridge across the Ohanapecosh River. A boardwalk loop trail takes the visitor by these old giants, which were growing when the Normans invaded England in 1066. This area was seriously affected by the floods in November 2006. A trail across the road from the parking lot leads to the picturesque Silver Falls, which is a mile roundtrip. The Eastside Trail will take the hiker to the Ohanapecosh Campground or up to Cayuse Pass. (SCR milepost 18.5) (Courtesy of NPS Rainier Archives.)

This entrance to the park serves visitors heading to Paradise from the south and east. Stevens Canyon Road was started in 1932 as a part of the around-the-mountain route and to connect the headquarters at Longmire with the newly opened services at Sunrise. Work was halted with the outbreak of World War II and was not resumed until 1951. The road was opened to the public in September 1957. (SCR milepost 18.6) (Courtesy of NPS Rainier Archives.)

Ohanapecosh Hot Springs was first noted by James Longmire during one of his explorations of the area in the 1870s. A tent camp and hotel were opened in 1912. The hotel and bathhouse seen here opened in the late 1920s. The completion of the road from Packwood to Ohanapecosh in 1933 allowed the springs to develop a regional reputation. (Courtesy of NPS Rainier Archives.)

The housekeeping cabins at Ohanapecosh Springs are seen here in the late 1930s. In 1931, the boundaries of the park were expanded to the east ridge of the Ohanapecosh Valley, bringing Ohanapecosh Springs within the park. The physician who operated the springs later founded the Mary Bridge Children's Hospital in Tacoma. This concession was independent of the Rainier National Park Company and lasted until 1961.

The first campground at Ohanapecosh was opened in 1923 by the forest service. It could be reached by trail from Longmire Springs or Packwood. A crude road from Packwood reached Ohanapecosh in 1925. The CCC expanded facilities between 1934 and 1940, including a forestry exhibit. This expansion of infrastructure at Ohanapecosh coincided with the closing of camping facilities at Longmire and Paradise. (Courtesy of NPS Rainier Archives.)

The East Side Road, or State Highway 123, connects the Mather Memorial Highway (State Highway 410) at Cayuse Pass to US 12 near Ohanapecosh. It is part of the proposed round-the-mountain route. Construction was started in 1931 and the road was opened on June 16, 1940. Shown here are the opening day ceremonies. (Hwy 123, milepost 19) (Courtesy of NPS Rainier Archives.)

Cayuse Pass is located at the junction of the Mather Memorial Highway and State Route 123. In the late 1940s and early 1950s, there was a small but popular ski area just off the ridge. The ski area closed with the opening of the better developed Crystal Mountain. (Hwy 123, milepost 16.4) (Courtesy of NPS Rainier Archives.)

The Mather Memorial Parkway (State Highway 410) closes at Silver Springs each winter because of the heavy snows in the Cayuse and Chinook Pass area. The Washington Department of Transportation strives to reopen the road by Memorial Day weekend. The road is closed around mid-November, depending on conditions. (Hwy 410, milepost 14.4.)

The Chinook Pass entry looks similar to others in the park. The intended effect is to have the visitor know that they are entering a national park. The first gateway was built by the CCC. The gateway is also a bridge that allows hikers and horses traversing the Pacific Crest Trail to safely pass over the highway. (Hwy 410, milepost 26.)

Tipsoo Lake & View from Chinook Pass

Lake Tipsoo is just below the summit of Chinook Pass to the west. This subalpine lake offers a great view of the mountain and an unusual view of Little Tahoma, a small peak to the east of the main mountain. The lake is frozen until early July. (Hwy 410, milepost 25.7.)

Mt Rainier and Tihsu Lake

Ellis 655

The 1931 expansion of the park's boundaries was, in part, in consideration of potential economic development of the lake area. On a clear day, visitors looking to the south may see Mount Adams, Mount Saint Helens, and, occasionally, Mount Hood. As camping has never been allowed at Lake Tipsoo, this is probably the CCC camp that was located here in 1936. (MMH milepost 68.4.)

Five

WHITE RIVER, SUNRISE, AND CARBON RIVER

Sunrise, Mt. Rainier National Park

The White River is on the northeast side of Mount Rainier. The north side of the mountain offers the visitor different views than those from Paradise and Longmire. Here, Little Tahoma is visible to the left (east). The Ingraham and Emmons glaciers, with Steamboat Prow, can be seen climbing up the flank of the mountain. Glacier Basin and the White River are visible in the bottom center.

Glacier Basin was the center of mining activities, with the first claims in 1897 and other claims surviving into the 1950s. The Mount Rainier Mining Company opened the Starbo Cooper Mine, and a rough road reached the valley from the Greenwater area. The company built this hotel between 1914 and 1917. A bunkhouse and other supporting buildings soon followed. The rusting mining equipment stood on the property for many years. (Courtesy of NPS Rainier Archives.)

The Yakima Park road was an extension of the White River Road and was built to bring visitors to the new Sunrise development built by the Rainier National Park Company. The road passes through thick forest as it rises 2,200 feet in elevation over a distance of seven and two-tenths miles to reach Sunrise Point. (SR milepost 12.6.)

7   THE SILVER FOREST NEAR SUNRISE LODGE   4A-H827

Silver Forest, which refers to a stand of trees that have died due to flood or fire, is a term that has been applied to several areas in the park. The original Silver Forest was near Longmire Springs. James Longmire was coming down from Paradise with a pack-train when several horses were stung by yellow jackets while passing through a grove of Alaskan Cedar. Knowing that a group of visitors would soon be using the same route, Longmire and a worker set out to burn the offending nest. Things got out of hand, and the grove caught on fire. The burnt wood was salvaged to build the National Park Inn and the Paradise Inn. This card is from the Sunrise area, where lightning caused a fire that burned several hundred acres. The Kautz Creek flood zone is a more recent Silver Forest.

MOUNT RAINIER

Rising 14,408 feet into the sky, Mt. Rainier is spectacularly beautiful, and the crowning triumph of the Evergreen State of Washington. Here it is only two hours from sea level to ski level.

This postcard was produced by the Washington State Progress Commission to promote postwar tourism. The card was one of a series distributed free to troops passing through the state. This card was mailed by a soldier serving at the Mount Rainier Ordnance Depot in 1943 to his sister in Biloxi, Mississippi.

RAINIER NATIONAL PARK

30-2405   HIGHWAY LEADING TO SUNRISE

The road from Sunrise Point to the Sunrise parking lot gives the visitor a great vista of the mountain. On a clear day, all one can see through the windshield is Mount Rainier. This postcard shows the meadows, along the road, full of wildflowers in August or September, and the islands of trees that are the basis for calling these areas parks.

36-461 Bus at Sunrise, Rainier Nat'l. Park.

Visitors are standing in a bus to get the best view of the mountain as they approach Sunrise. The red buses, or coaches, as they were called, departed from the Paradise Inn on daily tours. A restored coach is on display in season, in front of the old administration building at Longmire.

MT. RAINIER FROM YAKIMA PARK - WASH.

This view of Sunrise Village is from the early 1930s. Visible are the housekeeping cabins and lodge, which were opened in 1930. The photograph can be dated, as it does not appear that the first blockhouse or stockades are completed. The plan for Sunrise was to make it into a themed frontier village featuring cowboys and other such attractions. Trail names such as Sourdough are relics of the frontier theme.

This postcard from 1974 shows that the stockade and second blockhouse have been completed and that the housekeeping cabins have been removed. Behind the lodge, the damage that the cabins and paths have done to the meadows is still visible 70 years later. The Park Service has a continuing program to repair this kind of damage.

Sunrise was built by the Rainier Park Company with the intention of creating a "dude ranch" with horses, cowboys, and the like. One of the buildings has recently been updated to continuing service as an interpretation center where rangers are available to answer questions. The blockhouses are used for offices and as dormitories for park and concessionaire staff assigned to the area. (Courtesy of NPS Rainier Archives.)

The Sunrise Lodge was built by the Rainier National Park Company and opened in 1931 to serve day visitors. It has been remodeled several times to meet changing requirements. The main floor has a gift shop and dining room, and the upper floor has offices and staff quarters. (Courtesy of NPS Rainier Archives.)

This view of the lodge dining area shows that it was set up for cafeteria service. This proved to be popular with day visitors. There are no overnight accommodations at Sunrise. Sunrise tries to open each year by the Fourth of July, weather permitting, and closes at the end of September.

Stephen Tyng Mather was a San Francisco businessman, an early leader of the modern environmental movement, and a champion of the national park movement within the Department of the Interior. According to NPS biography sources, "Mather recognized magnificent scenery as the primary criterion for establishment of national parks. He was very careful to evaluate choices for parks, wishing the parks to stand as a collection of unique monuments." (Courtesy of NPS Rainier Archives.)

Washington State's highest peak, Mt. Rainier, as seen from Yakima side

This view of the White River and Mount Rainier is just the type of vista that Mather advocated preserving. He worked with multiple agencies in the State of Washington, the Forest Service, and private landowners to retain such views as the state constructed State Highway 410. Another of Mather's concerns was to limit logging in the upper White River Valley.

The opening of the Crystal Mountain ski area off of the Mather Parkway affected the park in two ways. The new facilities reduced public demand for ski lifts and towlines within the park and allowed other winter sports to develop in that area. As the new ski area and the park shared a boundary, concessions were made to allow the ski area to develop into what had been park land.

In the 1930s, the Park Service considered adding services and programs to the Carbon River side of the mountain. This drawing shows one proposal, which would have added a check station, gift shop, maintenance shops, and temporary staff housing near Mowich Lake. This and other plans for the area were never acted upon. (Courtesy of NPS Rainier Archives.)

The look of the mountain changes when it is viewed from different locations. This view from "Grinder Ridge" is somewhere near Mowich Lake. Clearly visible is Liberty Cap on the very top. Also less clearly seen is the cleft left by the Electron mudflow. One type of mudflow involves portions of a mountain slipping off the core without the intervention of a volcanic event. About 100 years before Columbus arrived in the Americas, the northwest side of the mountain slid, filling the Puyallup Valley. The debris field where the river leaves the park is over 100 feet thick. Subsequent flooding and erosion of the Puyallup River carried debris to Tacoma. There is the fear that a flash melting or release of a large amount of water from under a glacier could liquefy this debris field and bury Orting and Sumner. (Courtesy of Foothills Historical Society and Museum, Buckley, Washington.)

As part of the park's 100th anniversary in March 1999, communities around the mountain held celebrations. The towns of Wilkeson and Carbonado organized a classic car event. Here, the cars line up in Wilkeson as they prepare to drive to the Carbon River entrance. (Courtesy of Foothills Historical Society and Museum, Buckley, Washington.)

5944. Mount Rainier, Washington.

This early postcard shows a scene from somewhere near Indian Henry's on the west side of the park. The caption on the reverse of the card points out that at the time of the photograph, there were more acres of glaciers on Mount Rainier than in all of the Alps. As there were no concessions in this area, there was no need to produce postcards to promote activities.

Six

THE WONDERLAND TRAIL

Mount Rainier from Indian Henry's, Washington.   PHOTO BY ASAHEL CURTIS.

The Wonderland Trail is a loop trail of about 93 miles (the distance varies with alternate routes). The trail, which has an elevation gain/loss of over 20,000 feet, encircles the mountain in the forest-to-alpine zone. Hikers can join or exit the trail at several locations. Most people plan on completing the whole trail in 10 to 15 days, but some have been known to do it in less than 30 hours. This view shows the Longmire family's Camp Wigwam at Indian Henry's, which was the first night's stop for many of the earliest adventurers.

Mt. Tacoma from Mirror Lake, Washington.

Between Indian Henry's Hunting Ground and Tahoma Creek is Mirror Lake. For visitors prior to 1916, Mirror Lake was more accessible and, many believed, offered a better view than did Reflection Lake. As there were concessions at Indian Henry's and Longmire and none at Reflection Lake, photographers and postcard publishers had incentives to produce cards of Mirror Lake.

A crew of workmen cut a trail along a rock wall near St. Andrews Creek. When possible, slabs of rock are used on other portions of the trails. That is why drill holes are visible on some trail steps. Many groups volunteer to maintain the trails. Other trail camps on the west side of the Wonderland Trail include Pyramid Creek, Devil's Dream, South Puyallup, and St. Andrews/Klapatche Park.

The North Puyallup River Camp is 19 trail miles north of Longmire. The camp is located on the roadway of the abandoned Westside Road. The bridge across the north fork of the Puyallup is the last of the road bridges built on the west side. The camp is in a valley surrounded by soaring peaks.

This view of Mount Rainier is from Ipsut Pass, 35 miles from Longmire on the Wonderland Trail. This site is a short distance from the Mowich Lake Campground and about four miles from the Ipsut Creek Campground, the lowest point on the trail at 2,400 feet. Note how defined Liberty Cap is, on the top left of the mountain.

This is a view from Summerland Camp and is 66 trail miles from Longmire. Many hikers consider it one of the most spectacular spots on the mountain. Emerging from formidable lowland forests—the longest level stretch on the Wonderland—hikers find themselves on a mini-peak surrounded by alpine meadows. On one side, one towers over the Cascades facing the Central Washington grasslands. On the other side is the looming mass of Mount Rainier towering above.

Mt. Rainier   Indian Bar Camp   1375   July 1930

Indian Bar lies 72 miles from Longmire along a glacial river at the bottom of an alpine valley. Protected from the elements by hillocks and trees, the camper looks down the long, punishing staircase that lies either ahead or behind. To the other side, the trail runs across the top of a ridge with spectacular views of the mountain on clear days.

98

Seven

HIKES AND CLIMBS

In recent years, hiking the shorter trails of Mount Rainier has become the number one activity enjoyed by visitors. The park has 260 miles of maintained trails. Each visitor center, campground, and interpretive center has trails nearby. The trails are well maintained and marked, much of it done by volunteers. It is important for the long-term health of the park that visitors use only the marked trails. (Courtesy of NPS Rainier Archives.)

Mt. Rainier from Eagle Peak
Rainier National Park
2542

Eagle Peak is one of the oldest trails in the park. Edmund T. Coleman was a member of the Stevens-Van Trump attempt to first climb the mountain. He became separated from the others early in the effort and, while waiting for them, climbed Eagle Peak. The current trail is three and one-half miles long and leaves Longmire between the suspension bridge and community building.

COMET FALLS, RAINIER NATIONAL PARK, WASHINGTON. 72787

Comet Falls is on Van Trump Creek, above Christine Falls. From Longmire, the falls can be reached by taking the Van Trump Park Trail. The right fork of the trail will take the hiker across the Nisqually River, then up the Paradise River past Carter Falls to Narada Falls.

Van Trump Park is across the Nisqually Valley from Glacier Vista. Once at the park, the hiker has several route choices. One option is to take the five-mile Rampart Ridge Trail that overlooks the Kautz Creek Valley before returning to Longmire. Other destinations include Indian Henry's Hunting Ground and Mildred Point.

See Washington First.
The Switzerland of America.
Upper Nisqually Glacier and Mt. Rainier.

Photo by Curtis & Miller.

This 1920 postcard is from the Nisqually Vista Trail. The visitor can view all of the components of a glacier. The highest point, were the glacier originates, is called the glacier head. The glacier accumulation zone accounts for 60 to 70 percent of the surface area. The "snout" or terminus is the lowest point of the glacier and is where the creeks and rivers emerge from under the glacier.

Glacial moraines are rock fields that are formed by the deposits of material from a glacier and are exposed after the glacier has retreated. The terminus and moraine are dangerous. Rock and ice falls are constantly taking place off the face of the glacier. The boulders of the moraine are unstable and are not to be trusted to stay in place when stepped upon.

Easy Trails from Paradise Inn, Mt. Rainier National Park

The trails above the Paradise Inn and visitor center are well maintained, and, in season, busy. Visitors arrive from around the world. To ease the change in elevations, there are many stairs built into the trails. These stairs help the hikers and work to prevent erosion of the thin soils of the meadows.

Reaching Myrtle Falls requires an easy walk up Edith Creek from the Paradise Inn or the visitor center. There is a bridge for the Skyline and Golden Gates Trails that cross the creek. There is also a vantage point below the bridge, with the mountain looming in the background.

Myrtle Falls and Mount Rainier, Washington.

71284 SLUISKIN FALLS, MT. RAINIER NATIONAL PARK

Above Paradise on the Paradise River are the Sluiskin Falls. Gen. Hazard Stevens and Philemon Van Trump were the first to document a successful ascent of the mountain, on August 17, 1870. They were guided to the Paradise Valley by Sluiskin, a Native American guide who tried to talk the young men out of the attempt and then waited by the falls for their return.

Fairy Falls and Fairy Lake are part of the Stevens Glacier–Creek system. They are reached by taking the Skyline Trail to Sluiskin Falls, then taking the Paradise Glacier Trail. There is a branch off of this trail to Fairy Lake. Until the 1970s, Fairy Falls was listed as the tallest falls in the park. This postcard for the falls was mailed in 1929.

MOUNTAIN REFLECTED IN FAIRY LAKE

With the Stevens glacier retreat, the flow of water in the drainage declined. Now the falls and lake have all but disappeared from memory. This lake postcard was part of a 12-pack sold around 1932.

On the Skyline Trail, there is a branch that becomes the Lakes Trail. This loop trail connects Paradise to Reflection and Louise Lakes. The trail follows Mazama Ridge. A famous stop on the trail is Faraway Rock, which offers a panoramic view of the Tatoosh Ridge and Stevens Canyon.

Beautiful Washington.
Mount Rainier from Paradise Valley.

Reflection Lake, only several acres in size, is a favorite for many visitors. The rental boats are long gone, so the only obstacles to seeing a great reflection are the wind, rain, clouds, and fog. A loop trail circles the lake. Contrary to the photograph, there are no camping or picnicking facilities at the lake.

THE CASTLE AND PINNACLE PEAK

The Pinnacle Peak Trailhead is across from the Reflection Lake parking area. Pinnacle Peak and the Castle are part of the Tatoosh Range, which is, geologically speaking, much older than Mount Rainier. The trail is about a mile long to the gap. The very top of the peak requires special equipment and experience to climb. Every year, some visitors are seriously hurt trying to climb the last 100 feet. (SCR milepost 1.3.)

28-1499   On the Trail to Pinnacle Peak

This has been identified as a group of Explorer Scouts climbing the Pinnacle Peak Trail to camp and do trail maintenance. Much maintenance in the park is undertaken by volunteer groups such as this one. Experience has shown that large groups are more prone to damage the meadows than smaller groups. Backcountry permits help to limit group size.

Nature coasting was an activity popular with previous generations. It started with "tin pants" made of heavy canvas and waxed to provide waterproofing. Waxing the seat of the pants had the same effect as waxing skis or surfboards. Tin pants are still available and are popular with foresters and others who work in wet woods where normal cloth would tear. On some of the guided hikes, visitors were issued tin pants. When a suitable glacier or snowfield was found, the pants were donned, the visitors sat down (as shown in both of these images), and then they slid down the hill as on a toboggan. Some cards indicate that this was done on the slopes of the Tatoosh Range.

Horse rides were once a popular activity. A trip to Pinnacle Peak would take most of a day. Master plans for the park developed in the 1960s limited the use of horses in the park. No single reason led to this decision. Rather, there were several concerns, including the introduction of disease into the wildlife, the introduction of nonnative plant seeds found in animal feed, grazing on the meadows, the placement of trail steps, and the insufficient strength of backcountry bridges to accommodate a horse's weight.

The Naches Peak Loop Trail is 4.5 miles long and leaves from the Lake Tipsoo entrance arch. It takes the visitor past subalpine lakes and highland meadows. In late August and September, the area is ablaze with fragrant wildflowers. Part of the trail is on the famed Pacific Crest Trail. The Naches Peak Loop Trail is best done in a clockwise manner in order to face the mountain.

The Glacier Rim Trail is to the south of the main parking lot at Sunrise. It extends eastward to the Silver Forest, and to the west where it joins the Burroughs Mountain Trail. It overlooks Glacier Basin, and was one of the popular short horseback rides that left from the lodge. There are six other trails crossing or branching off of this route.

The Sunrise Trail extends the Sourdough Ridge Trail further to the east to Sunrise Point, then down off the ridge to Sunrise Lake. Several different trails branch off to lakes and other points of interest. Going out from Sunrise, the view is of the central Cascade Range from Snoqualmie to White Pass. On the return view, there is the mountain.

On the Burroughs mountain trail near Yakima Park

Burroughs Mountain is at the end of the ridge that forms Sunrise. The five-mile, round-trip hike gains an additional 1,400 feet of elevation, but the visitor is rewarded with an unimpaired view of Mount Rainier, which is so close that it cannot all be seen without a turn of the head.

The Mount Fremont Lookout is reached by taking the Burroughs Mountain Trail, then branching off at Frozen Lake. The lookout was one of a series that surrounded the mountain. It offers views of Grand Park and other parts of the park, with a view of the Olympic Mountains in the far distance.

Grand Park is one of the larger park areas in the national park. It is on the Northern Loop Trail that connects the Carbon River area to Sunrise. In 1965, a fire caused by lightning burned several hundred acres. Current regulations allow fires to burn unless they threaten infrastructure, endanger historic sites, or obstruct visitors and personnel from leaving the park, among other criteria. (Photograph by Glen Powell, ranger naturalist.)

These early hikers are looking down on Mowich Lake from Knapsack Pass. This is in the northwest corner of the park. There are a number of shorter hikes in the area. This photograph was taken by Asahel Curtis, a professional photographer who documented park scenes for many years. He was one of the founders of the Mountaineers and photographed many of their activities.

Mt. Rainier reflected in Lake Eunice

Lake Eunice is reached by a spur off the Tolmie Peak Trail, which leaves from the Mowich Lake trailhead and branches off the Wonderland Trail at Ipsut Pass. Lake Eunice, to the northwest of Mowich Lake, is at the foot of Tolmie Peak (named for the first European to reach the area, in 1833).

Mother Mountain runs southwest to northeast between the Mowich and Carbon Valleys. It is several miles long and has an elevation of over 6,400 feet for much of its length. The crest is very steep and craggy. Large snowfields are found on the northern exposures.

Mount Rainier, Washington.

The top of Mount Rainier has acted as a magnet for a portion of the population since it was first discovered and explored. There is no evidence or oral history that Native Americans attempted to summit. The first known expedition to the mountain took place in 1833, when there were fewer than 500 people in the state. This view, from the rim of the crater, is looking across the snowfields toward the summit.

With the completion of the National Park Inn at Longmire, the Tacoma Eastern Railroad marketed travel to the mountain to groups. One of the first groups to come to Mount Rainier was the Mountaineers of Seattle. Formed in 1906, this group of adventurers was interested in exploring the peaks and wilderness around Seattle. They soon adopted Mount Rainier as one of their favorite haunts.

P 819 - Mt. Rainier Looking into Cr

This aerial view of the summit is from the southeast, looking to the northwest. The summit is the goal of the 9,000 to 14,000 climbers who set out each year. A little more than half of these climbers achieve the summit. Liberty Cap, in the center of the photograph, is at 14,112 feet. Point

114

Success (14,158 feet) is on the left. Columbia Crest (14,410 feet) is hard to identify in this image but is on the far edge of the crater. The crater is clearly visible on the right. Little Tahoma Peak is in the lower center. There are some 35 different routes to the top, from all sides.

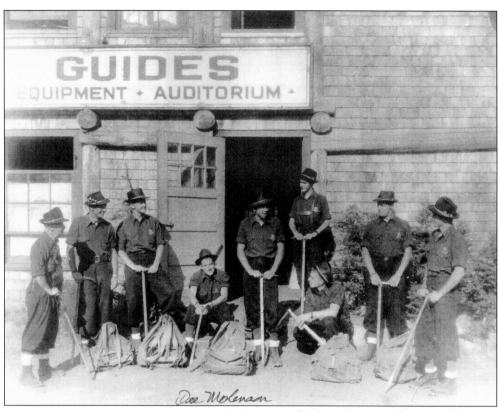

Dee Molenaar

For most climbers, the start of a successful expedition is meeting with their guide. The guides are young men and women who not only know the different ways to the top, but can read the conditions of sky and ice so as to keep their party safe. They teach the novice the skills to travel across ice and snow and to move at high elevations.

CAMP MUIR CABIN, Elevation 10,000 feet, Rainier National Park

Camp Muir, named for famed conservationist John Muir, is at the 10,000-foot elevation above Paradise. The camp is used as a staging area for groups going to the summit. Here, the climbers arrive in the afternoon, have something to eat, and take a nap. They leave early in the morning on their attempt. Coming down off the mountain, Camp Muir is used as a resting spot.

For safety reasons, climbers are often roped together so that they can support each other across crevasses and other difficult terrain. This early view shows a party of climbers learning how to connect to the line. Many mountaineering techniques have been developed by guides and climbers on Mount Rainier. (Courtesy of Linda Lewis.)

This party of climbers is exploring the upper reaches of an unidentified glacier. The rope work has been described as primitive. The photograph is by Asahel Curtis, professional photographer and first chief guide for the Rainier National Park Company. The climbers' clothing appears to be from around 1915, so it is believed that this is a party of Mountaineers from Seattle.

These climbers are exploring large blocks of ice on the Emmons Glacier above Camp Schurman, which is located at the upper point of Steamboat Prow. It is reached by a trail coming up from Glacier Basin. The Winthrop Glacier and Curtis Ridge can be seen above the climbers' head.

Glaciers, Mt. Rainier National Park

These climbers are exploring a bergschrund on the Nisqually Glacier above Gibraltar Rock. The bergschrund is a specific type of crevasse that is formed either when the ice cap of a mountain flows off the top and then down the steep sides, or when a glacier starts at a wall or ridge. In most cases, this is the highest and largest crevasse of a glacier.

RAINIER NATIONAL PARK

30-2258   A BERGSCHRUND NEAR THE SUMMIT   1A289

ICE BRIDGE ON NISQUALLY GLACIER, RAINIER NATIONAL PARK.

This group is being guided by Alma Wagen (far left), a teacher at Stadium High in Tacoma. After serving as an assistant guide for several years, she started serving as a guide in 1918. She led John D. Rockefeller Jr. and many others on their climbs. The ice bridge may have been formed when a boulder froze in the ice and then melted out.

AN ICE WALL NEAR THE SUMMIT

This party is practicing climbing a glacier wall with a ladder. In addition to the ladder, the wall is being scaled by digging toe and hand holes in the face with an ice ax. The climbers then use toe picks on their crampons to scale the wall. Crampons are attachments to climbing boots that allow climbers to walk on hard ice without slipping. A pick extends from the toe of the boot.

28-1653   SUMMIT CLIMBING PARTY ABOVE THE CLOUDS   1136-29

Climbers pause to look around after having climbed above the clouds. This view is to the east, with the peak of Little Tahoma in the lower right. In a short time, the party will arrive at Disappointment Cleaver, at the 12,500-foot level.

This group is pausing at the rim of the crater at the top of Rainier for a celebratory photograph. Most groups do not spend much time on the summit. There is a log book to be signed and sights to be seen. The top is often cold, cloudy, and windy. Climbers need to start heading down before the sun causes the ice to melt and conditions to become slippery.

Eight

OTHER THINGS TO SEE

Mount Rainier National Park has a lot to see and do. If necessary, much of it can be done from the roadside or on short walks on easy trails. There is always the mountain to see, and its appearance is always changing. Among the park's attractions are the rainforest and subalpine meadows; lakes, rivers, and waterfalls; an abundance of wildflowers; and animal life. These bird-watchers are participating in a national bird count near Longmire. (Courtesy of NPS Rainier Archives.)

One unusual sighting near Mount Rainier occurred on June 24, 1947. Kenneth Arnold was looking for the location of a Marine transport plane that had crashed the previous December. Just before 3:00 p.m., at 9,200 feet, he saw a flash in the distance like sunlight off of a mirror. The single flash soon became a string of nine, flying very fast and in formation at a high altitude. He thought they were coming from a new military aircraft, but he could see neither engines nor tails. In Arnold's initial descriptions, he likened their movement to saucers skipping on water. At one point, he timed their passage between Mount Rainier and Mount Adams and calculated speeds in excess of 1,700 miles per hour. Arnold was interviewed by several newspapers, which reported his sighting and started calling the mysterious objects "flying saucers." There were at least 16 other reported sightings by other pilots and observers that day. The postcard calls these planes C-111 Fortresses, which is confusing. Fortresses usually had a B-17 classification.

A book published in black and white cannot adequately convey the splendor of the wildflowers of Rainier. The many variations of white, red, yellow, pink, blue, and green seem to stretch for miles. In fact, they do! Starting in July, the meadows come alive with acres of wildflowers. Coming to life are, first, avalanche lilies, then paintbrush, lupine, asters, pasqueflower, and many more.

MT. RAINIER NATIONAL PARK, NEAR SEATTLE -- TACOMA, WASHINGTON   THE MILWAUKEE ROAD

Visitors are likely to see wildlife in the park, but these animals are more shy than their cousins at other parks. Deer may be seen in all regions of the park. They are most active around sunrise and sunset. Most often, if one deer is spotted, several others will be nearby.

The major problem animals have in the park is with people. Visitors feeding wildlife may cause the animals to no longer fear people and to become lazy and cease to seek their normal diet. This may lead to a failure to store food for winter, malnutrition, and/or aggressive behavior. When animals become aggressive toward people, they must be destroyed or relocated. (Courtesy of NPS Rainier Archives.)

Black Bear, Mt. Rainier National Park

By the early 1960s, bears were becoming a significant problem. The Yogi Bear image had people visiting national parks to feed the bears. In many places, bears had lost their fear of humans and roamed campgrounds in search of an easy meal. The Park Service responded by conducting public education, installing new garbage dumpsters, and moving garbage dumps out of the parks. Backcountry users have special instructions for safeguarding food.

The mountain goats in the park are the descendants of colonies that fled south ahead of the last ice age. The goats have found a suitable home in several areas of the park where they can find their favorite lichen and need not fear predators like cougars. The postcard does not indicate the location of these goats, but this may be on the south face of Satulick Mountain, south of Indian Henry's.

The Cascade fox, like the mountain goat and marmot, is another refugee from the ice age. The species, considered threatened, is found only in the higher elevations on the Cascade peaks. In fact, one was seen and documented crossing the glacier at the top of Mount Rainier. In winter, they may be seen, near dusk, at the Paradise parking area. (Photograph by Sara Yates; courtesy of NPS Rainier Biology.)

Mount Rainier National Park was established in 1899. In the 113 years since, four park rangers have died in service to the public. On August 12, 1995, climbing rangers Sean Ryan (left, age 23) and Philip Otis (below, age 22) left their base at Camp Schurman in the evening to assist an injured climber near the 13,200-feet level of the Winthrop glacier on the north side of the mountain. A subsequent inquiry determined that improvements were needed in safety standards, training, equipment, and communications. Family members of the two men have written books and articles about the incident and its impact. The photograph of Sean Ryan on the left was taken as he summited Mount Rainier in July 1995. (Left, courtesy of Michael Gauthier; below, courtesy of Todd Otis.)

Law enforcement ranger Margaret Anderson was shot and killed by a park visitor on January 1, 2012. The shooter was being sought by authorities for a shooting outside the park. Anderson had established a roadblock preventing the shooter from reaching visitors at Paradise. Anderson was 34 and had worked at Mount Rainier for three years. She was survived by her husband, who is also a park ranger, and two young children. (Courtesy of NPS Mount Rainier Information.)

Climbing ranger Nick Hall died on the mountain on June 22, 2012. He was assisting in the evacuation of a party of four climbers from Waco, Texas, off the Emmons Glacier. Two members of the climbing party had fallen into a crevasse and were injured. The rescue helicopter was leaving the area when Hall fell more than 3,000 feet down the glacier. (Courtesy of NPS Mount Rainier Information.)

Discover Thousands of Local History Books Featuring Millions of Vintage Images

Arcadia Publishing, the leading local history publisher in the United States, is committed to making history accessible and meaningful through publishing books that celebrate and preserve the heritage of America's people and places.

Find more books like this at
www.arcadiapublishing.com

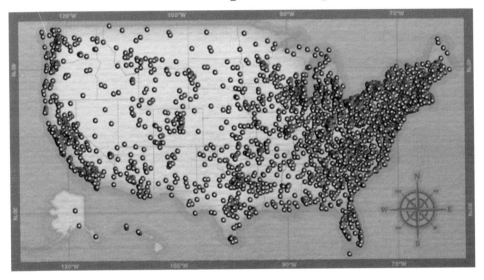

Search for your hometown history, your old stomping grounds, and even your favorite sports team.

Consistent with our mission to preserve history on a local level, this book was printed in South Carolina on American-made paper and manufactured entirely in the United States. Products carrying the accredited Forest Stewardship Council (FSC) label are printed on 100 percent FSC-certified paper.

MADE IN THE

USA